10/98

The Origin of the Universe

Andres Llamas Ruiz

Illustrations by Luis Rizo

Sterling Publishing Co., Inc.
New York

Illustrations by Luis Rizo
Text by Andrés Llamas Ruiz
Translated by Natalia Tizón

Library of Congress Cataloging-in-Publication Data

Llamas Ruiz, Andrés.
    [Origen del universo. English]
    The origin of the universe / by Andres Llamas Ruiz ; illustrations
by Luis Rizo.
        p.   cm. — (Sequences of earth & space)
    Includes index.
    Summary: Describes briefly the most widely accepted scientific
explanations regarding the origins of the universe, the birth of
stars, and the formation of the planets.
    ISBN 0-8069-9744-3
    1. Cosmology—Juvenile literature.   2. Stars—Formation—
Congresses.   3. Planets—Origin—Juvenile literature.   [1.
Cosmology.   2. Universe.]   I. Rizo, Luis, ill.   II. Title.   III.
Series: Llamas Ruiz, Andrés.   Secuencias de la tierra y el
espacio.   English.
QB983.L53   1997
523.1´2—dc21   96–37980
                                                                        CIP
                                                                        AC

1   3   5   7   9   10   8   6   4   2

Published by Sterling Publishing Company, Inc.
387 Park Avenue South, New York, N.Y. 10016
Originally published in Spain by Ediciones Estes
©1996 by Ediciones Lema, S.L.
English version and translation © 1997 by Sterling Publishing Company, Inc.
Distributed in Canada by Sterling Publishing
%Canadian Manda Group, One Atlantic Avenue, Suite 105
Toronto, Ontario, Canada M6K 3E7
Distributed in Great Britain and Europe by Cassell PLC
Wellington House, 125 Strand, London WC2R 0BB, England
Distributed in Australia by Capricorn Link (Australia) Pty Ltd.
P.O. Box 6651, Baulkham Hills, Business Centre, NSW 2153, Australia
Printed and Bound in Spain
All rights reserved

Sterling ISBN 0-8069-9744-3

Table of Contents

The First Ideas

For centuries, scientists wondered how and when our universe was formed. In some ancient cultures, people believed that the sun and the moon were friendly gods, with the sun providing light and warmth during the day and the moon lighting up the darkness of the night.

Eventually, early astronomers made the first scientific observations about the sky, although they often made mistakes. In ancient Greece, for example, they believed that the earth was a sphere at the center of the universe.

In the 16th century, a Polish astronomer named Nicolaus Copernicus proved that the earth, as well as the other planets in our solar system, revolved around the sun. In the 1780s, scientists discovered that the millions of stars seen from the earth formed a galaxy called the Milky Way.

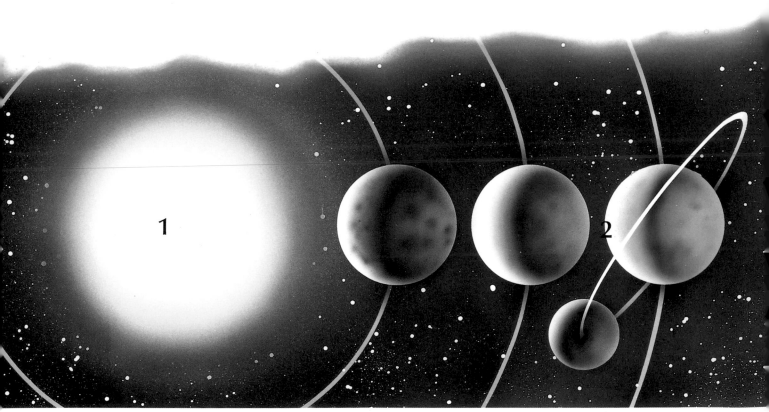

This is a sketch of the universe as Copernicus envisioned it. His ideas encountered strong opposi-tion from the "official" science of the time, which represented the opinions of the Catholic Church.

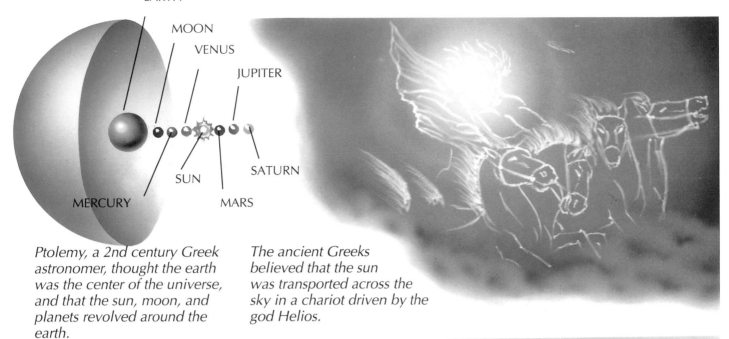

Ptolemy, a 2nd century Greek astronomer, thought the earth was the center of the universe, and that the sun, moon, and planets revolved around the earth.

The ancient Greeks believed that the sun was transported across the sky in a chariot driven by the god Helios.

Large megalithic stone blocks are found in England at Stonehenge. Some scientists believe they were used as astronomical observatories.

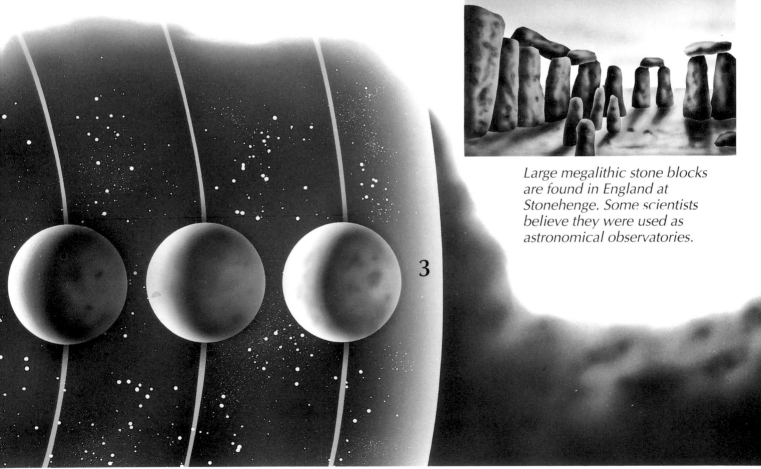

1. The sun is the center of our solar system and the planets revolve around it.

2. The earth is a planet that revolves around the sun.

3. Immobile sphere of fixed stars.

Before the Explosion: The Beginning

The universe is constantly expanding as galaxies separate from one another. This means that if we went back in time many centuries, we would reach a point where we would find all the galaxies packed into one very small area.

Many scientists believe that the earth was formed as the result of an explosion that occurred approximately 15 billion years ago.

This explanation is called the Big Bang theory. According to this scenario, all the matter and energy in the universe were concentrated in a very small spot, which measured in the millions of degrees. There was then an explosion called the Big Bang and the universe started to expand in all directions.

No scientist has been able to explain exactly what existed before the explosion occurred, although some believe that there was nothing before our universe was born.

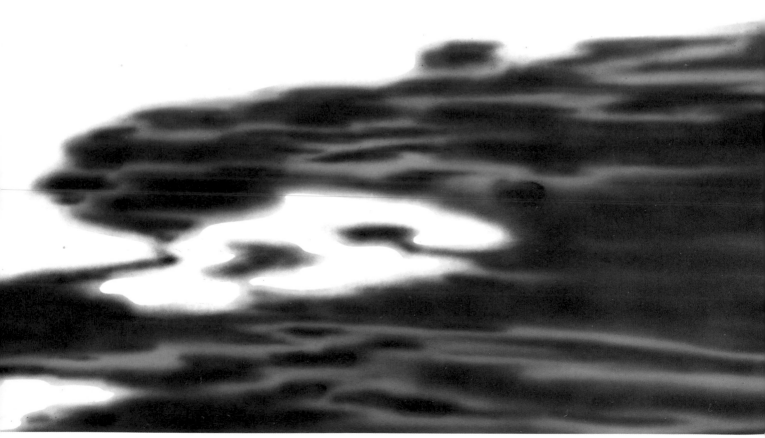

The Big Bang theory is the explanation of the creation of the universe that is most widely accepted by current scientists. However, this theory poses many questions. For example, what existed before all the matter and energy were gathered together in one place?

1. In the beginning, all the matter and energy in the universe were concentrated at one point.

Thanks to the invention of the telescope, a 17th century Italian astronomer named Galileo Galilei began to explain the movement of the stars.

For early astronomers, the moon was a fascinating mystery. Today, there exists a very detailed map of its surface, with its craters and "seas"— dark regions with large lava-filled craters.

2. The temperature was very high. Some scientists calculate that a mere 1/43 of a second after the explosion, the temperature registered billions and billions of degrees Fahrenheit. One second after the Big Bang, the temperature had "cooled down" to 18 billion degrees F.

3. Around the area of the explosion, absolute darkness and emptiness prevailed.

The First Second of the Big Bang

In order to estimate when the explosion took place, astronomers have considered the current expansion rate of the universe and have reached the conclusion that the Big Bang took place about 15 billion years ago!

As you already know, at the moment when the explosion occurred, all the matter and energy of the universe were concentrated in a very small spot, which caused the temperature to soar into the billions of degrees! After the explosion, as the universe quickly expanded, it cooled down at great speed. Approximately one-millionth of a second after the Big Bang, the temperature registered about 18 trillion degrees F. But as the seconds ticked away, the temperature dropped abruptly: By about 1.5 minutes after the explosion, it read "only" 1.8 billion degrees F. As the universe cooled off, subatomic particles called quarks formed the protons and neutrons that would later combine into the nucleus of an atom. Just one second after the Big Bang occurred, cosmic matter was already forming from protons, neutrons, and electrons.

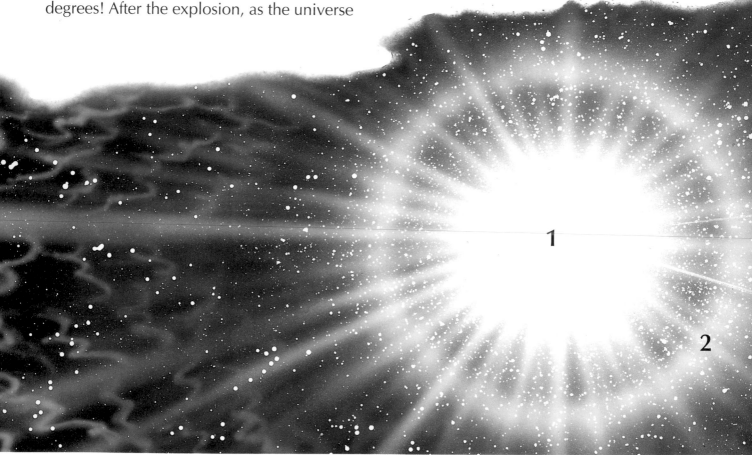

At first, the entire universe was formed by a fireball made up of hot, dense gas that quickly cooled down as it expanded. The hot spots that remained formed the stars.

1. The universe expanded at tremendous speed during the first moments after the great explosion.

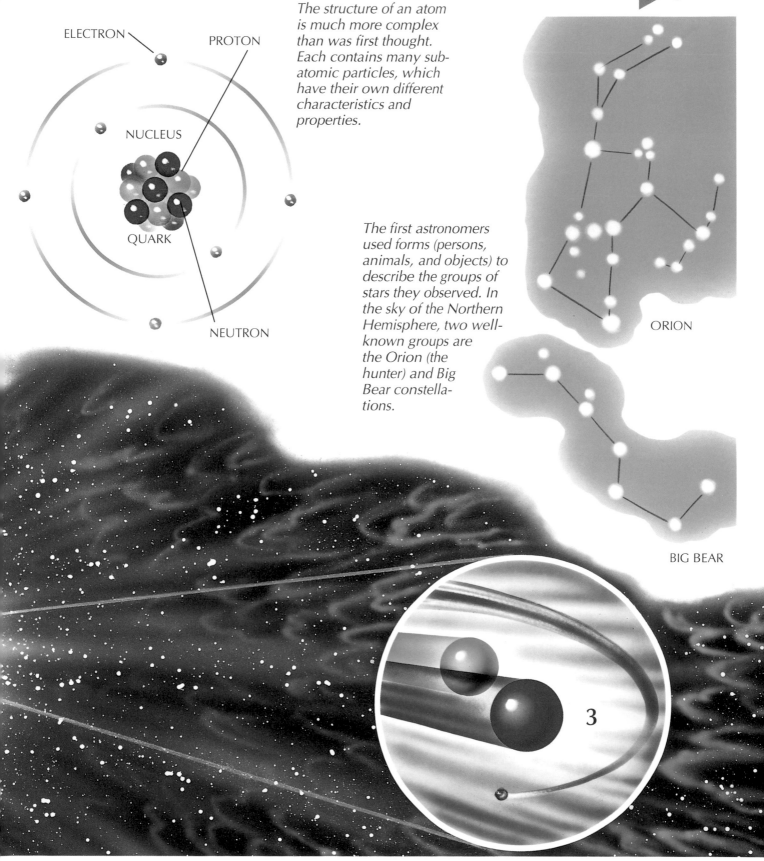

ELECTRON

PROTON

NUCLEUS

QUARK

NEUTRON

The structure of an atom is much more complex than was first thought. Each contains many sub-atomic particles, which have their own different characteristics and properties.

The first astronomers used forms (persons, animals, and objects) to describe the groups of stars they observed. In the sky of the Northern Hemisphere, two well-known groups are the Orion (the hunter) and Big Bear constellations.

ORION

BIG BEAR

3

2. The temperature dropped quickly (although it continued to register at millions of degrees Fahrenheit).

3. Subatomic particles (protons, neutrons, and electrons) appeared. Soon, they formed the universe's first atoms.

The Universe Lights Up

Approximately 100 seconds after the Big Bang, the temperature of the cloud of cosmic matter dropped to "only" 1.8 billion degrees F. As a result, small subatomic particles gathered and, it is thought, within 3 minutes of the Big Bang, the first chemical elements began to form. Matter as we now know it had begun to appear!

One million years later, as the universe continued to develop, gas began to contract in large groups called protogalaxies. These would in time form the universe's many diverse galaxies, one of which is ours—the Milky Way. The closest galaxy to ours is Andromeda, which is "only" 2.3 million light-years away.

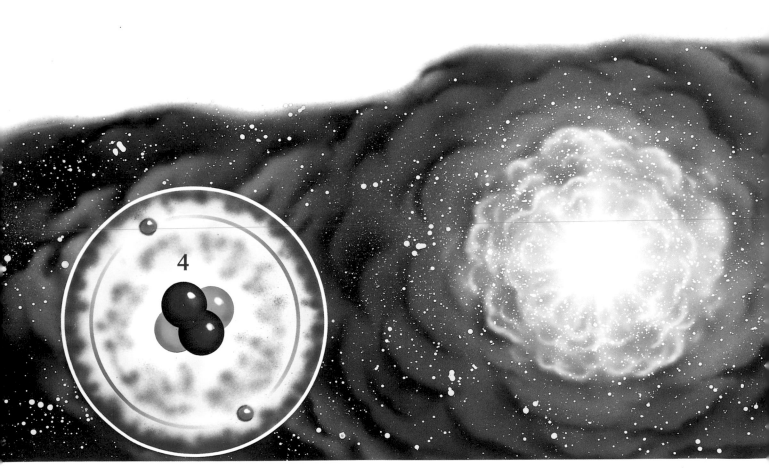

Three hundred thousand years after the explosion, the universe began to light up.

1. About 2 minutes after the explosion, helium began to form inside an enormous cloud.

HORSEHEAD

PLEIADES

A nebula is a cloud composed of gas and cosmic dust. It can be seen when the star or stars inside it heat the gas enough to glow (emission nebula) or if the nebula itself reflects the light of the stars (reflecting nebula). They are also visible when they darken the light of faraway objects (dark nebula). The Horsehead nebula represents the dark type, the Pleiades represents the reflecting type.

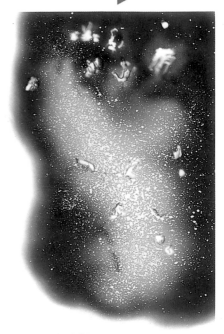

MAGELLAN

The great Magellanic Cloud is an irregularly shaped galaxy.

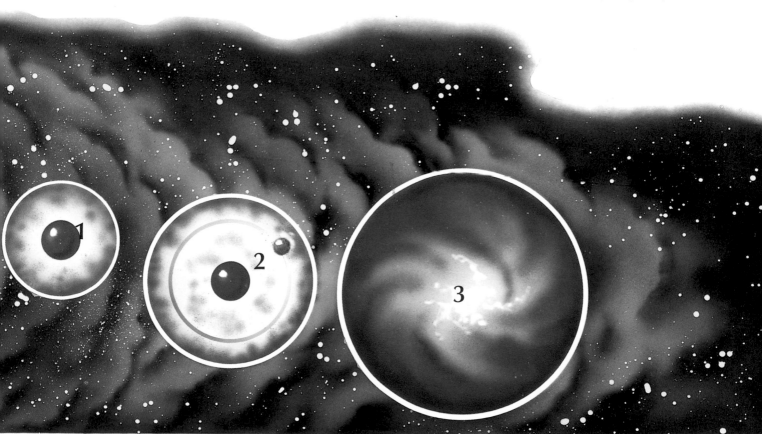

2. The first hydrogen atoms appeared.

3. In some regions, gas, made up of helium and hydrogen, started to contract to form protogalaxies that would become galaxies.

4. One-fourth of all the matter in the entire universe condensed into helium. Even today, the ratio remains the same.

Clouds That Will Become Galaxies

Between 100,000 and 1 million years after matter first appeared, atoms of helium and hydrogen began to group together to form gigantic clouds of gas called cosmic nebulae. These nebulae gradually developed into galaxies and stars, giving the universe its current form.

Although a nebula contains some helium, it is made up mostly of hydrogen, which has a density of only six atoms per square inch. Despite such low density the total mass of these enormous clouds is one hundred to one million times larger than the mass of our sun.

Our galaxy, the Milky Way, was formed 7 to 12 billion years ago. The shape of the galaxies can vary greatly. Ours is a spiral.

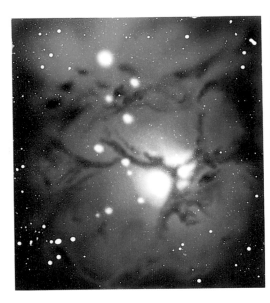

Clouds also possess solid dust particles made up of helium and hydrogen. They are 160 times denser than water. Their extreme density and heat cause fusion, which makes highly packed atoms explode, converting mass into energy.

The center of the nebula (**A**) starts to contract to form "protostars" (**B**) that will create new stars.

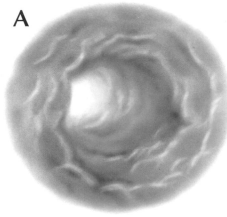

A

B

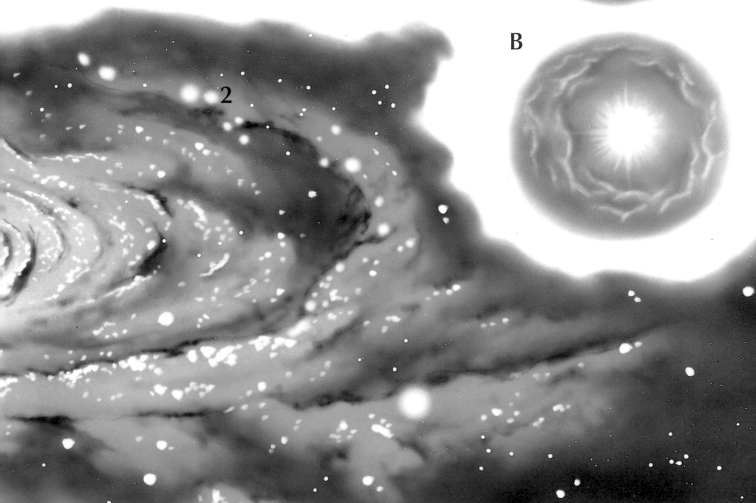

2

1. Nucleus of the spiral galaxy with old stars.

2. Cosmic dust in the arm of the spiral; dust reflects light from the young stars.

3. Young stars in the arm of the spiral.

4. Glowing nebula in an arm of the spiral.

The Stars Are Born

After the Big Bang explosion, the first stars were formed inside gigantic rotating nebulae, or clouds, of dust and gases. Gravity caused some of these clouds to contract and increased their speed of rotation. When this happened, the central areas became very hot (due to the continuous gravitational pull). At a certain point, the temperature caused a series of reactions that would create a new star. The process was a slow one, which took millions of years to complete.

When the temperature at the center of the cloud reached many millions of degrees F, hydrogen atoms began to collide with each other until they formed helium atoms. This process is called "nuclear fusion," a reaction that releases an enormous amount of energy in the form of heat and light.

Our closest star, the sun, was formed approximately 6 billion years ago and will continue to exist for another 7 billion years.

1. First, there was a huge nebula of gas and cosmic dust.

2. As the nebula began to contract, its center heated up.

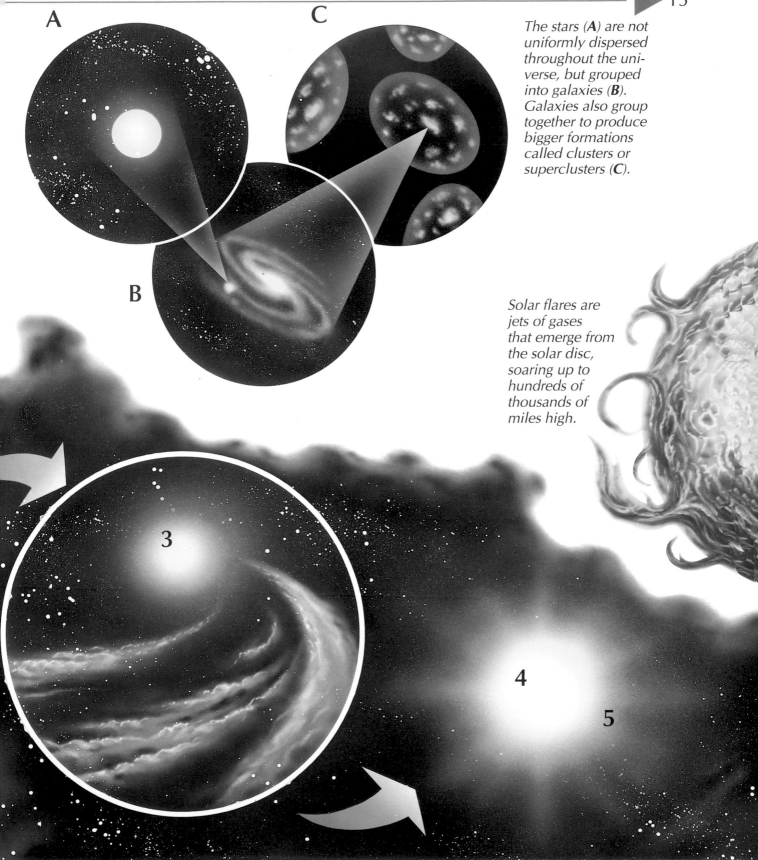

The stars (**A**) are not uniformly dispersed throughout the universe, but grouped into galaxies (**B**). Galaxies also group together to produce bigger formations called clusters or superclusters (**C**).

Solar flares are jets of gases that emerge from the solar disc, soaring up to hundreds of thousands of miles high.

3. The center became very hot and the cloud flattened.

4. The center of the cloud exploded to create the sun.

5. Sunlight was emitted in all directions, illuminating the planets around it.

The Color of the Stars

Stars shine because they are very hot. They obtain energy from the nuclear reactions that occur inside them. But have you noticed that their color differs?

Stars send light waves, but their light changes as the star moves. As a star approaches us, its light appears whiter. When it moves farther away, its light takes on a red cast.

During the 1920s, astronomers were surprised to discover that most known galaxies emitted red-toned light. Why? Because most galaxies are traveling away from us at great speed. Those galaxies that are farther away travel faster, even tens of thousands of miles per second!

As the universe expands, groups of galaxies separate from one another. You can see here the variations in the colors of light we receive from stars of other galaxies, depending on their distance from the Milky Way.

Stars emit their own light. Their color depends on the star's surface temperature.
• Blue stars are the hottest, with an average temperature of 45,032°F.
• White stars have an average temperature of 10,832°F.
• Yellow stars have an average temperature of 8540°F.
• Red stars are the coldest, with an average temperature of 4940°F.

1. When a galaxy travels at great speed, it creates short blue waves in front of itself and leaves long red waves behind.

2. The speed at which a group of galaxies travels away is calculated by observing the redness of its stars.

Stars Change

Although all stars look like dots of light that seem about the same size, they can be very different from each other. Some look like the sun; others are much smaller or much larger.

The life span of stars varies and their development depends mostly on their initial mass. For example, the biggest stars have the largest hydrogen cores; the more hydrogen a star has, the more energy it produces. The cores of larger stars grow very hot and quick

ly "burn" all of their combustible matter. All stars—including yellow ones, such as the sun—expand when they run out of combustible matter and become red giants. They are called red giants because, as they increase in size, their outer layers cool down and glow with a red light.

After millions of years, the red giants are depleted of energy. From then on, their nuclei start to cool, and they fail to produce enough heat to counterbalance the gravitational forces. Then, they collapse in on themselves. This causes their outer layers (cold and red) to warm, exploding violently to form supernovas.

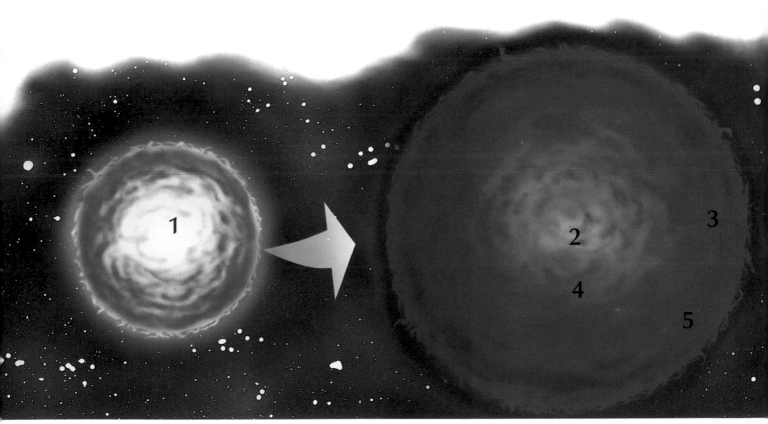

The star changes in appearance over millions of years as its combustible matter burns.

1. A yellow star burns for millions of years.

2. It expands as it runs out of combustible matter.

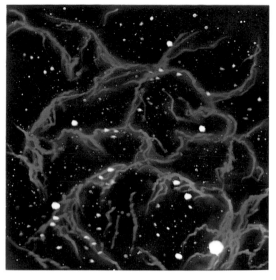

You can see here the remains of a supernova. This is a shell made of gas that quickly travels far away from the area where the star exploded. For some time, the supernova will glow in the sky as brightly as a galaxy.

Neutron stars are formed from the nuclei of atoms that remain after the explosion. Neutron stars are very small (6 to 9 miles across) and consist only of neutrons. They are so dense that one little spoonful of their matter can weigh up to a billion tons!

6

3. Its outer layers cool down and emit a red light. The star becomes a red giant.

4. The star's core starts to cool down and the star fails to generate enough heat to counterbalance gravitational forces.

5. The star collapses onto itself and the outer layers warm up.

6. The star explodes to become a supernova.

New Elements Are Formed

Approximately 75 percent of all the existing cosmic matter is composed of hydrogen, while helium forms 24 percent of the total. All other chemical elements together make up only 1 percent of the matter. Almost all cosmic matter is hydrogen. Why? Hydrogen atoms are the simplest of all existing atoms. Each is composed of a nucleus with a positive charge (proton) and an outer layer with a negative charge (electron).

However, there are up to one hundred different chemical elements in nature that can either remain isolated or combine with other compounds. Where did all of these elements come from? All chemical elements, except hydrogen and helium, are formed from hydrogen in reactions caused by high temperatures inside the stars. When the stars explode, they emit totally new elements in different directions throughout space.

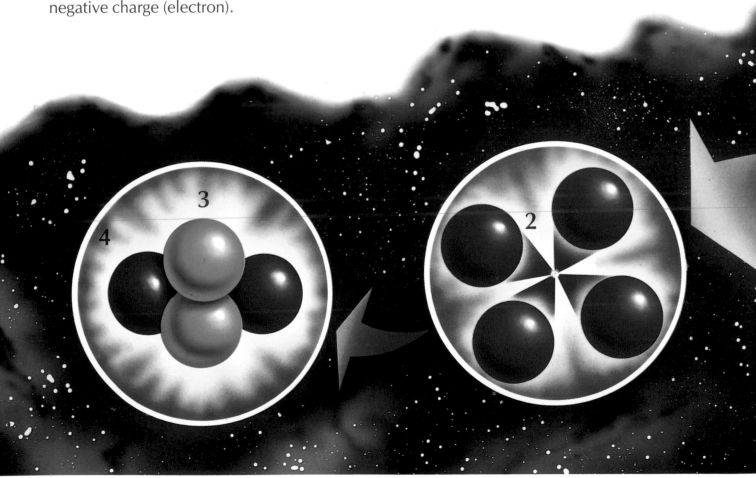

Inside stars, such as our sun, the nucleus is formed as hydrogen converts to helium through nuclear fusion. A great amount of energy is released during this process.

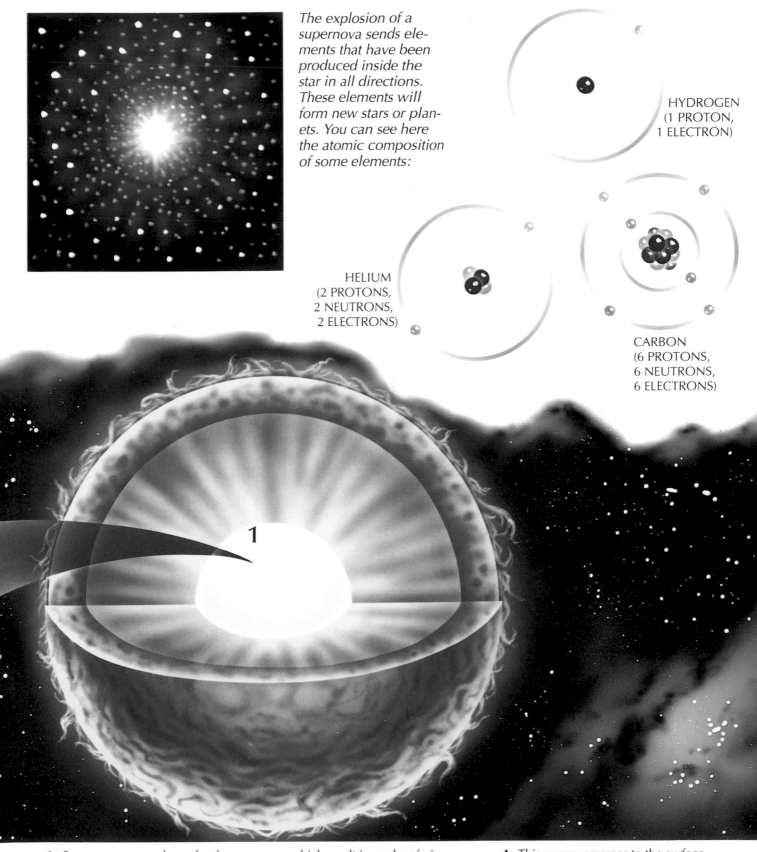

The explosion of a supernova sends elements that have been produced inside the star in all directions. These elements will form new stars or planets. You can see here the atomic composition of some elements:

HYDROGEN
(1 PROTON,
1 ELECTRON)

HELIUM
(2 PROTONS,
2 NEUTRONS,
2 ELECTRONS)

CARBON
(6 PROTONS,
6 NEUTRONS,
6 ELECTRONS)

1

1. Stars are composed mostly of hydrogen.

2. Due to very high temperature and pressure, hydrogen atoms collide, which result in nuclear fusion.

3. As a result, helium is produced, and energy equal to an atomic explosion is released.

4. This energy emerges to the surface of the star in the form of light and heat.

Planets Are Formed

During ancient times, astronomers were intrigued by the stable glow of what seemed to be a few "nomad stars." In reality, these "stars" were the five planets closest to one another in the solar system (Mercury, Venus, Mars, Jupiter, and Saturn). Our solar system contains nine large planets and hundreds of small ones, which are called asteroids. All travel at different speeds around the sun in an elliptical orbit.

The planets were formed by the same cloud of dust and gases that contracted to create the sun. Asteroids come from matter that condensed into small pieces when the larger planets were formed.

Comets and meteors can also be seen in the night sky. Comets appear for a few weeks or months; meteors can be seen for only a second or less.

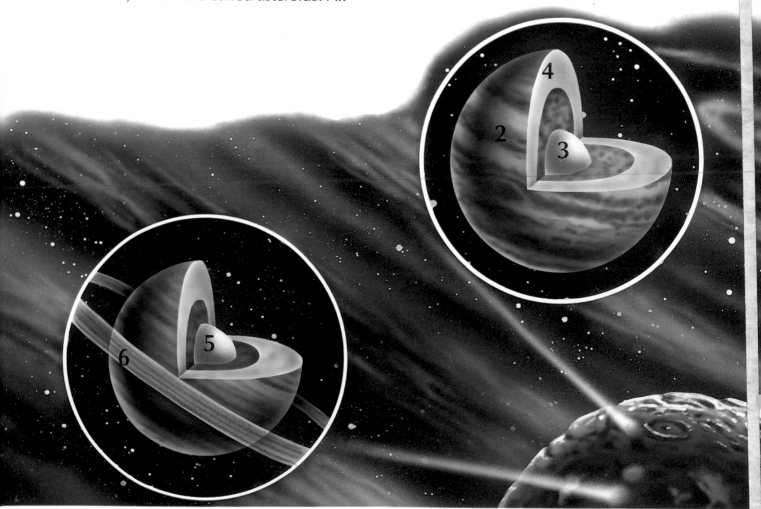

Planets differ from one another in shape and size as well as in composition.

1. Mercury is the closest planet to the sun.

2. Jupiter is the biggest planet in the solar system.

The asteroids and comets that we can see from the earth are the remains of the nebula that formed our solar system 4.6 billion years ago.

A meteor shower occurs when the earth passes through a stream of dust particles left behind by a comet. These particles warm up when they enter the atmosphere and appear as a glowing line of light.

DUST PARTICLES
THAT REFLECT
SUNLIGHT

TAIL

CRUST

NUCLEUS

ICE

STRUCTURE OF A COMET

3. Astronomers believe that Jupiter has a small core of rock surrounded by a mantle of liquid metallic hydrogen.

4. In its outer layer, there is a liquid hydrogen mantle.

5. Saturn has a nucleus of rock and ice.

6. It has a system of rings 328 feet thick that can extend up to 261,000 miles from its surface.

An Expanding Universe

In 1929, American astronomer Edwin Hubble was surprised to discover that galaxies constantly traveled away from our Milky Way.

Galaxies belong to large groups called clusters. Each one of these groups is distant from each other. Astronomers have discovered that the farther away galaxies are from our Milky Way, the faster they separate.

What does it mean to say that galaxies are separating? It simply means that the universe is expanding! The universe becomes bigger and bigger as the space between the different galaxies increases. In fact, no one knows for sure how big the universe is.

Some astronomers estimate that the universe contains approximately 100,000 million galaxies, each of which contains approximately 100,000 million stars!

In the 1920s, Edwin Hubble finally proved that the fragments of light we see in the sky (and what the scientists call nebula) are systems of stars similar to our galaxy.

1. There are three main types of galaxies:

a. Elliptical (oval-shaped).

The cluster of galaxies to which our Milky Way belongs is rather small, since it only contains about twenty galaxies. However, in the Virgo constellation, which is 50 to 60 million light-years away, clusters include thousands of galaxies!

Observed from an enormous distance, the universe could be compared to a cluster of soap bubbles. Galaxies would form the outer rim of the cluster; the bubbles would be hollow inside and differ in size from one another.

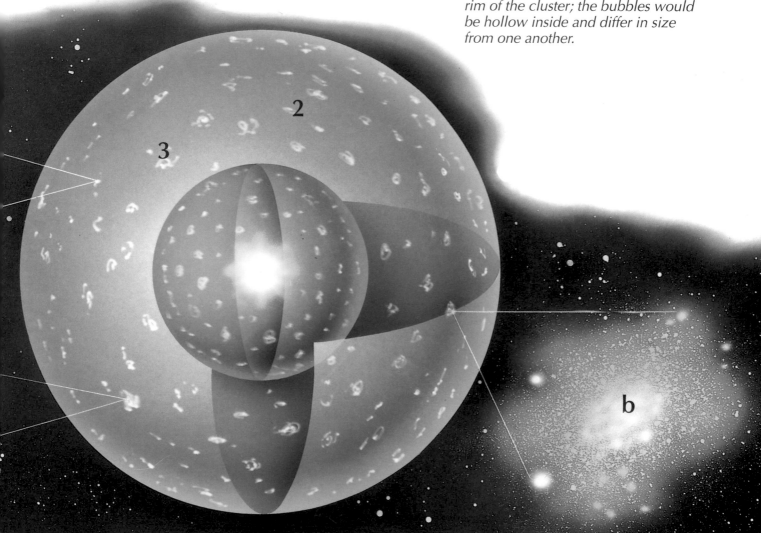

b. Irregular (no defined form).

c. Spiral (with arms that originate from the nucleus).

2. The smallest galaxies contain only 100,000 stars.

3. The biggest galaxies may contain up to 3 billion stars.

Echoes of an Ancient Explosion

Did you know that astronomers can still detect the remains of the Big Bang? As the universe expanded and cooled down, light waves created during the great explosion changed over millions of years. Gradually, they became longer and were transformed into radio waves of great amplitude that can be detected from the earth. This means that scientists can still listen to the "echo" of that first explosion!

The Big Bang theory is supported by the discovery of slight background radiation that comes equally from all directions of the sky. Astronomers believe that this radiation is the residue of that faraway first explosion. They also believe that the small variations observed in the temperature of cosmic background radiation prove the primitive changes in universal density that created the first galaxies.

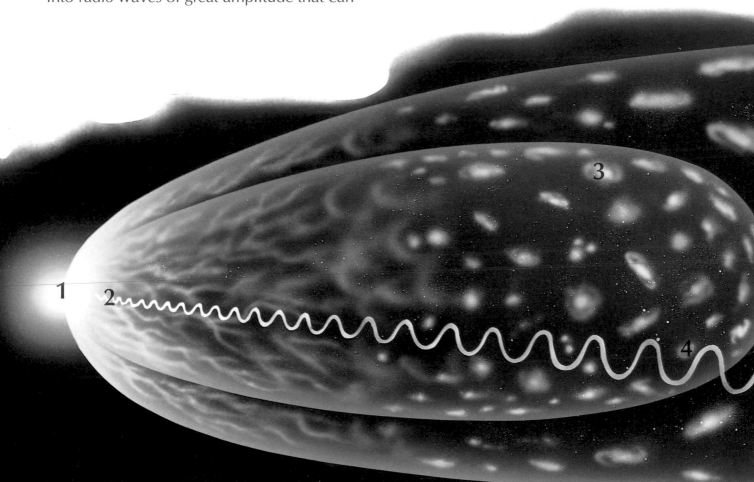

The universe has been continuously changing in appearance since its beginnings after the Big Bang. Since then, it has also grown in size.

1. Very hot, expanding gases.
2. High-energy radiation caused by a temperature of 5432°F.

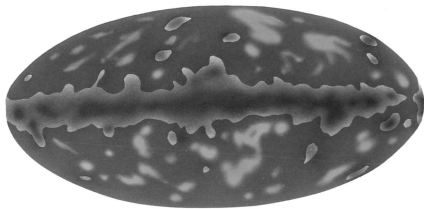

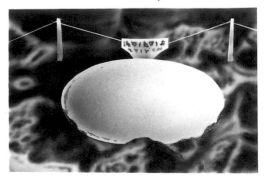

On the map, the dark blue represents background radiation (-518°F) caused by the remains of the Big Bang. Red indicates radiation emitted by our own galaxy.

The antenna of the radio telescope in Arecibo, Puerto Rico, sits in a valley and measures 1000 feet wide! This is the largest in-ground radio telescope in the world.

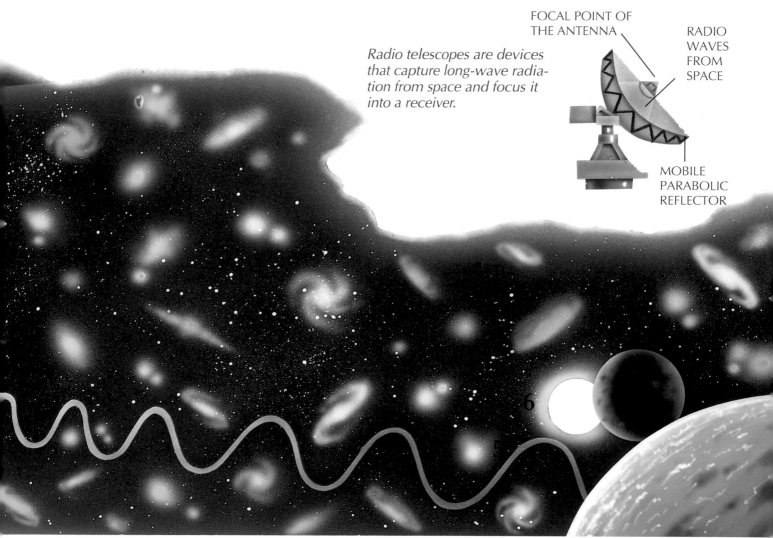

Radio telescopes are devices that capture long-wave radiation from space and focus it into a receiver.

FOCAL POINT OF THE ANTENNA

RADIO WAVES FROM SPACE

MOBILE PARABOLIC REFLECTOR

3. Appearance of the universe, between 1 and 5 billion years after the Big Bang.

4. Contracting gas clouds.

5. Low-energy radiation caused by a temperature of -518°F.

6. Our current universe. Billions of years have passed since the explosion.

Seeing the Past in Space

Light travels through space at a speed of 186,000 miles per second. If a star is 5 light-years from us, its light will take 5 years to reach us. The distances in space are so great that they are hard to imagine. For example, Andromeda, the closest galaxy to our Milky Way, is "only" 2.3 million light years away. This means that its light takes more than 2 million years to reach us, or rather that what we are currently seeing as light was generated over 2 million years ago. When we look at the stars, we are actually looking at their past!

The observed light of the farthest known quasar, the brightest object in the universe, takes 12 billion years to reach us. When that light was first created, our universe was just beginning to form. Can you imagine what might have happened to the quasar since it began to emit the light we now see? The next time you raise your eyes to the stars, remember that the stars you are looking at may have disappeared billions of years ago.

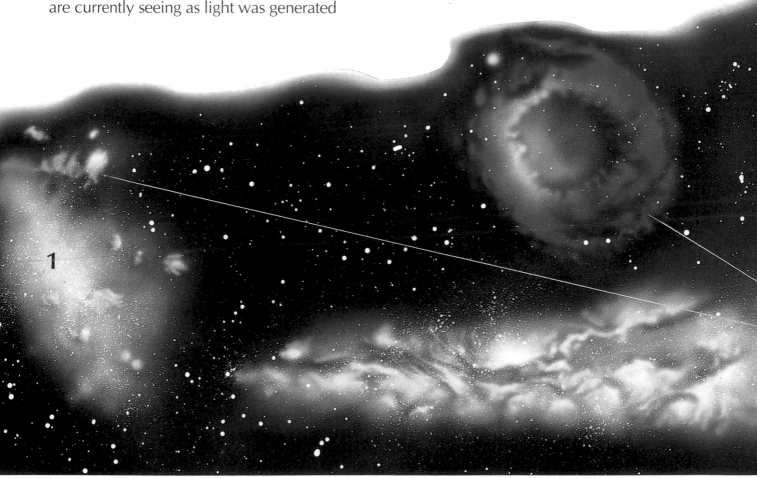

1

One light-year is equivalent to approximately 5.8 trillion miles, since it is the distance that light travels in 1 year. Distances in space are enormous. Our solar system only measures about 12 light hours in diameter (about 8 million miles). Our galaxy, the Milky Way, measures about 70,000 light-years!

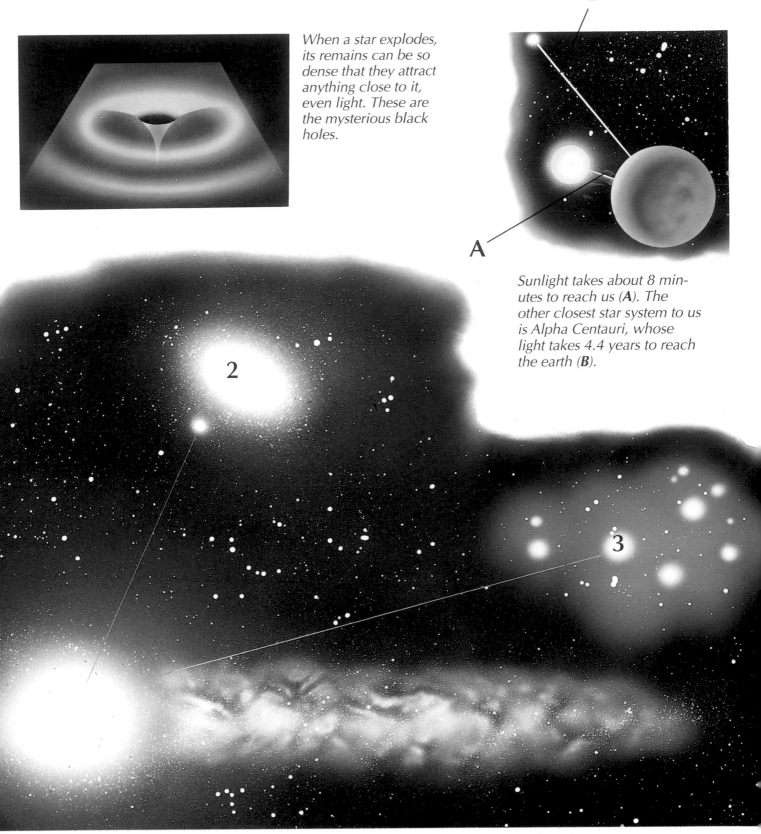

When a star explodes, its remains can be so dense that they attract anything close to it, even light. These are the mysterious black holes.

B

A

Sunlight takes about 8 minutes to reach us (**A**). The other closest star system to us is Alpha Centauri, whose light takes 4.4 years to reach the earth (**B**).

2

3

1. New stars are still created from dust and gas clouds in space.

2. However, if one star is created very far away from our galaxy, it is possible that its light will not reach the earth until many millions of years later.

3. The light of some stars was emitted billions of years ago.

And Then What?

Scientists do not know what will happen to the universe in the future. According to the Big Crunch theory—one of several unproved scientific theories—the universe will never stop expanding, or maybe its own gravity will gradually halt its expansion. Some astronomers believe that the universe could then shrink and contract until it explodes again to create a new Big Bang. It is even possible that the universe has suffered several Big Bangs periodically.

The theory of the Oscillating Universe states that the universe will not continue to expand forever. According to this theory, the speed of expansion will diminish due to the influence of the galaxies' gravitational pull. At some point, expansion will stop and gravity will again pull together different galaxies to form a single mass that will warm up, explode, expand, and so on, in an infinite cycle.

Some scientists think they have found proof of a reduction in the universe's expansion. They theorize that, according to their calculations, the current cycle may still have 100 billion years before the universe contracts again to a single point.

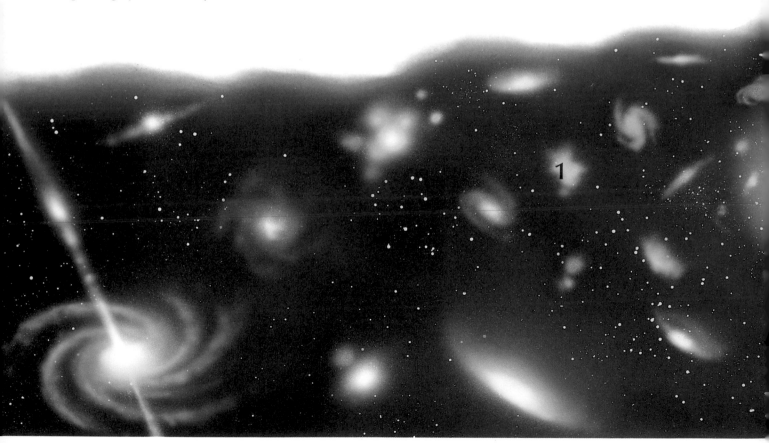

Scientists do not yet agree about the universe being open or closed. If it is open, it will continue to expand forever. If, on the other hand, it is a closed system, it will stop expanding at some point in the future and contract again.

1. Galaxies are pulled together by their gravitational forces.

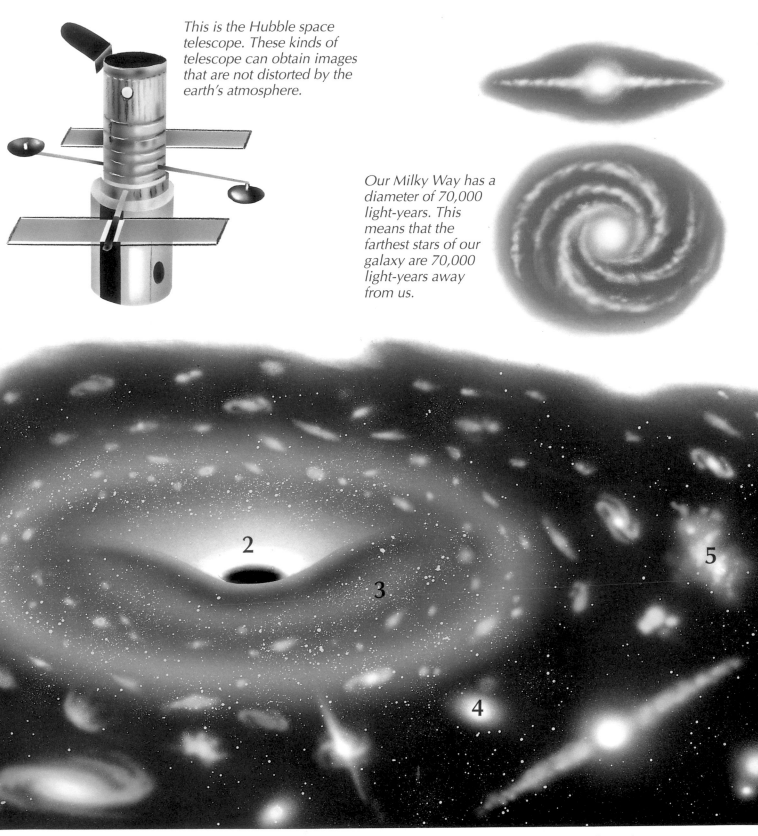

This is the Hubble space telescope. These kinds of telescope can obtain images that are not distorted by the earth's atmosphere.

Our Milky Way has a diameter of 70,000 light-years. This means that the farthest stars of our galaxy are 70,000 light-years away from us.

2. Matter and energy contract.

3. An explosion disperses matter and energy in all directions.

4. The universe expands continuously.

5. According to the Big Crunch theory, the universe stops expanding and the galaxies pull together once more. The cycle begins again.

Glossary

Billion: Equivalent to one thousand millions: 1,000,000,000.

Comet: Small, icy body about 10 miles in diameter. A comet travels in a long, eccentric orbit.

Density: Mass divided by volume equals density.

Electron: Subatomic particle. Electrons have a negative charge. They are 1840 times smaller in mass than one proton.

Galaxy: Group of stars, gas, and cosmic dust held together by the force of gravity.

Light-year: The distance light travels in a vacuum during the course of a single year. Since light travels at 186,281 miles per second, each light-year represents 5.88 trillion miles.

Meteor: Also called a shooting star, a meteor is the streak of light seen when a fragment of rock or metal traveling at great speed through space burns when entering the earth's atmosphere.

Mythology: History of gods, demigods, and heroes of ancient times.

Proton: A positively charged particle contained in the nucleus of the atom.

Quasar: The brightest objects in the universe, these compact objects look like stars. They are thought to be the center of active galaxies whose energy sources may be black holes.

Star cluster: Group of stars that are formed at the same time. Galaxies also group in clusters and superclusters.

Subatomic particles: Smaller than atoms, they include electrons, protons, neutrons, and so on, that form atoms.

Supernova: Spectacular explosion of a star at the end of its life. It can shine as brightly as an entire galaxy.

Index